A word of warning from the author, this book contains some material that may be disturbing to some readers. It contains vivid imagery of an attempted suicide with a firearm and some aspects of child abuse. It is based on a true story. The names of the characters have been changed.

C. Price

christian.price2012@gmail.com
Find me on Facebook: Christian Price

When an Angel Intervenes

By:

Christian Price

CHAPTER ONE

Opening the closet door, Bill had a hard time deciding what shirt would complement his blue tie. Would it be the long sleeve white or the short sleeve white? The forecast called for snow showers with a wind chill in the low twenties. The short sleeve shirt was shoved aside and the long sleeve shirt taken from the hanger. Bill stood in front of a mirror trying to get the tie just so. It had served faithfully through many weddings and funerals. Erika said it made his eyes stand out; she thought his blue eyes were his best feature. Pulling out the only sport coat in his wardrobe, he laid it across their bed. Down the hall a hair dryer was working to dry Erika's hair as she made final preparations. Reaching under their bed, he pulled out a pair of black dress shoes that were coated in very fine layer of dust; they were rarely used. Making use of his hand to wipe the dust away, he heard the sound of the hairdryer abruptly quit working.

A muffled complaint could be heard through the closed door followed by a brisk yank of the bathroom door. Erika yelled down the hall, "Great. Bill the hairdryer just went. I need a new dryer this week."

"I think you look great. I love that tussled hair look. It's a nice look on you." Bill yelled back down the hall.

"No. Looking like a smelly, wet sheep dog is not a good look for me and I'm not going to your twenty year reunion sporting that look. When Belinda gets here, will you ask her if she'll run back across the street to her house and bring back her hairdryer and let me use it for the night?"

Recognizing his wife's tone, it was not a question but thought it was worth a try "I'd rather not have to ask the neighbor if we could borrow her hairdryer."

"Please."

The issue weighing on Bill's mind was not that Erika wanted him to ask the neighbor if they could borrow a hairdryer, it was he did not want to attend his high school reunion that night. It had been twenty years since they had graduated and that long since he had seen any of them. It had not been a good time in his life, and it would be best to keep the past where it belonged and to not dredge it up and rehash things over cocktails. Out of one eye he saw their two year old son Brady proudly run down the hall with a bright red marker in his hand. Duly noted was the fact the cap was missing from the marker.

"Erika! Brady is heading your way with a marker in his hand. I think he has been drawing pictures because the cap is missing."

"Where did he get the marker from? Please go see where he drew pretty pictures ok? I'm trying to finish with my make- up while I wait for Belinda to get here." The front door bell rang, "There she is! Don't forget to ask her to run back and grab her dryer; please. Did you see what Brady was drawing on?"

Walking out of their bedroom to go look for Brady, there standing in the hallway and proudly showing his daddy his new treasure. Brady's face and legs were covered in red with the marker held high. Afraid to see how creative the boy had been on his sister's bedroom wall, Bill noticed a few squiggly lines had been hastily drawn with all the care a two year old can put into wall art. His son stood and smiled up at his father all very proud of himself. It was hard to be upset. A sigh released some frustration as he removed the marker from Brady's small chubby hand and offered a firm "no". Brady's four year old sister Anna was busy playing with a farm set grandmother had given her as a birthday present. Erika's mother enjoyed lavishing her grandchildren with gifts. Anna loved the farm animals and Erika's mom was a big help in making sure the family had nice gifts for birthdays and Christmases. It was all he could do to keep the basics provided for so that little bit helped, a lot.

"Honey, please get the door. Did you see where Brady colored and will you check on Cayden? See if he is still down for his nap. Speaking of markers, when was the last time you checked in on Anna?"

"Brady has marker on his face and legs, he left us pretty pictures on Anna's bedroom wall, and I don't know where he got the marker from. Anna is playing with her farm. I'll check in on Cayden when I get back from letting Belinda in."

Stepping over the baby gate with all the skill of an Olympic Sprinter clearing a hurtle hoping to reach the door before it rang again, Bill reached the door and opened it as Belinda had her hand on the bell.

"Hey sorry, it's hectic upstairs. Thank you so much for coming over tonight and keeping an eye on things for us tonight."

"No problem. Glad I could help out. You kids need to get out of the house more often. Besides you have the cutest kids, and I made them cookies. It'll be fun."

"Thanks, those cookies look good. Come on in. I almost forgot would it be too much trouble to ask if Erika could borrow your hairdryer hers just broke?"

Erika yelled down to them from the upstairs hallway, "Hi Belinda! Thanks so much for helping us tonight and did my husband ask you for your dryer?"

Yelling over Bill's shoulder Belinda called back through the front door "He sure did sweetie; I'll just run back home and get it. Be back in two seconds. Here will you take these for me?" She passed the cookies to Bill, turned, and headed back down the walkway.

"Oh, hey Belinda, I'm sorry I didn't get a chance to lay out salt or clear the walkway. It wasn't supposed to start snowing until late this evening."

"No problem. You don't have two teenage sons to help out like I do. I'll send them over to clear your sidewalk. They're cheap; they work for food. You go on and finish getting ready; we'll be back in a moment."

"Ok, thanks for everything. I'm going to go open the gates and release the hounds. They'll be ready for you when you get back."

"I'm sure my chocolate chip cookies will take the bark out of any fussy ones. My cookies are world famous. Besides, how do you think I'm going to coax two boys loafing on the couch to come back here and clean your walk way. They work for food and accomplish a lot when chocolate chip cookies are involved."

Closing the front door, good neighbors like Belinda and her husband Dave, made this little corner of the world a nice place to live. Dave drove a long haul truck and was gone many days at a time. Bill kept an eye on their place while Dave was on the road; he would want someone to keep an eye on Erika and the kid's if he were gone frequently.

Going back up the stairs and stepping over the baby gate, a sweet voice called from their bedroom, "Honey, will you please come in here and reach up on to the top shelf and get my shoes in the pink box?"

Going into their bedroom, he reached up to the top shelf, and without any warning, a sharp tearing sensation tore through his left chest. Wincing in pain and reaching under his left arm to use his right arm as a splint, he applied pressure to reduce the tearing sensation.

Taken back by that episode, he sat at the foot of the bed to rest for a moment. That hurt; that was a nasty one, he thought. You'd think after twenty years I'd be used to it every time it gets cold and damp. I swear it feels like someone is taking a razor and is trying to slice and dice me from front to back."

"I'm sorry your chest is bothering you. Have you taken something for the pain? I hate to see your chest hurt you like that"

"No, it just started. I wish there was time for a heating pad. It would feel great over the old scar tissue"

Gingerly standing up, so as to not have that old scar send another wave of pain shooting through his chest and feeling confident the worst had past, Bill headed down the hall to the bathroom to the medicine cabinet. Pulling a bottle of aspirin out of the cabinet and tossing two in his mouth, he chased it with a hand full of water from the bathroom sink.

Erika yelled down the hall, "Well, you know what they say about chicks?"

"No. What do they say?" walking back to the bedroom to get his sport coat on.

Sliding her arm around his neck she whispered in his ear "Chicks dig scars."

"Is that why your married me?"

"No. I married you because of your money."

That made him smile. After seventeen years of marriage, she was his everything. It would be nice if he was able to provide a better standard of living for her. She deserved it. She was a wonderful person.

Many of the men on his job site spoke in a degrading tone about their wives. That was a conversation he avoided. Not only was she his wife, but she was also his friend.

"Ok, I'm ready whenever you are. How long before you're ready?"

"As soon as Belinda gets back with the dryer I can dry my hair. Maybe another twenty minutes."

A few minutes passed. The front door opened, and Belinda let herself in.

"Boy it's really starting to come down; doesn't look like it's starting to stick, though."

"I think they should cancel the reunion." Bill said to Belinda as they sat on the couch in the living room waiting for Erika to finish getting ready.

"They can be awkward. We went to ours a few years ago," Belinda replied. "Everyone looks so different; it really shows you how fast time flies. It really made me think how fast those twenty years had gone by. Then I got to thinking, if those twenty were over in a snap, how fast would the next twenty blow by?"

"Yeah, it's hard to believe twenty years is gone. It feels just like yesterday I was in school with them."

At the top of the stairs, Erika worked on getting her earrings in. She asked if Bill would warm up the van while she offered Belinda advice on how to keep a lid on things. They would only be gone a few hours.

Stepping outside armed with a broom and a few brisk wisps, the van was cleaned off. He climbed in the van and turned it on. There was a loud metallic tap from the motor. Broken hair dryers and broken vans, the sound of the hairdryer dying sounded like a cheap fix, this not so cheap. As the oil started to circulate through the motor, he really hoped it would quiet down. Since the last time he drove the van.

Watching as the windshield wipers moved back and forth across the windshield, he thought to himself, "This is all I need. I can't afford a stupid hairdryer; now this. It feels like some days someone knows I am teetering on the edge, and they are just trying to just shove me over the edge. I wish the work would come back in like it used to." Bill patted the dashboard gently. It had been a good vehicle over the years. They just needed it to last awhile longer.

New homes were just not going in at the rate they used to. Many of the buildings in the area had newer roofs so there was little work to be had in replacing the existing roofs. With the motor warming up, the loud metallic tap went away. At least it was trying to work with Bill. With the van motor quiet, he got out and headed into the house. Walking across a cleared walkway, he thought he should take a moment and appreciate small things like good neighbors and a van that was trying to hold on.

Stomping on the welcome mat and going in to find his little ones running around with cookies in hands, he helped Erika on with her coat as she offered a few more words of wisdom on what Belinda could expect. Hugs and kisses were given to the little ones, and a final thank you to their neighbor. The couple was shooed out of the house with assurance that if anything should go wrong Belinda would call them. Climbing into the van and its welcoming heat, Erika asked Bill how his chest was feeling.

"Better, the aspirin seems to be working."

"When you started the van did you notice how noisy it was?"

"Yeah, I'm going to try using another brand of oil to see if that will quiet it down. I think it should. We've kept up with the maintenance; I'm sure we will get another fifteen thousand miles out of it before we have to do something."

"I hope so. It makes me nervous. I'm sure we'll be fine, but I can't imagine if we had to take on a car payment"

Heading out to the twenty year Park City High School Reunion Class of 1988, the roads were reasonably clear and the salt trucks had been up and running since the morning pre-treating the roads. At this point, they were working to stay on top of things keeping the busy weekend Christmas Shopping Traffic flowing to the regional malls. Christmas carols played on the radio as the windshield wipers lazily swished back and forth doing their part to clear snow.

"Hey I have an idea. Instead of going to this reunion let's find a place that serves a nice steak or maybe splurge and have lobster" Bill suggested.

"What? We paid for these tickets. A moment ago, we were just talking about how slow this year has been. We can't afford to spend money on tickets and not use them, let alone go out and have lobster."

"I know. A steak dinner and a night on the town with you sounds like a good time." resigned Bill. "Having dinner with people I haven't seen in twenty years? Not such a good time"

Slowing down to let a plow truck past, he held his breath as the plow truck sprayed salt and small rocks all over their van. One small salt pebble thrown into the motor may be all it took to send the van into a death spiral. The salt truck passed and the van was still running.

Turning up the radio for one of his favorite Christmas Carols, "I like this one."

"I'm talking to you don't turn up the radio." Erika continued "Going for Lobster is a wonderful idea and I'll certainly take you up on that idea after the Christmas Season. I think it's a little late in the game to try and change our plans. We ordered these tickets several months ago. I think something else is going on. Do you mind telling me what's *really* going on?"

Turning the radio back down, he tried to focus on the road and on his thoughts, "I don't want to go. Not everyone has fond memories of their past. Not all of us want to just sit around and celebrate our childhood. I've not walked those halls in twenty years and a lot of things happened to me back then. Those things need to stay in the past and not be brought back out like some play thing. We have plenty on our plates to deal with, we don't need to go around and mess with old memories. Christmas is in two weeks. Who has a reunion this time of the year? It's a stupid idea in my opinion."

"I'm sorry. I thought it was a wonderful idea." Erika replied "I'm sure there are some of your classmates that won't be able to attend because of the time of year they chose to have it. There'll be plenty of time for us to go out and have a night out. This only comes along every ten years. I thought I was your first and only. Are you worried we may run into an old girlfriend of yours?" Erika joked trying to add a little light humor to the growing tension that grew with each passing mile as the school grew closer.

"I don't think that was funny. How long have you and I been

married? You know I don't have any ex-girlfriends."

"Sorry. You don't have to be so snippy. I hope you aren't going to be this grouchy all night and ruin our night."

The rest of the trip remained quiet. The shadow of the school peered through the murky night. The school lot was cleared of snow. Finding a place to park, Bill parked the van and shut the motor off. With the engine no longer running, the silence just hung in the air like a hazy, hot, humid July afternoon. Erika sat with her arms folded across her chest staring out the window. After seventeen years of marriage it was easy to recognize what her body language was communicating. It said *I'm getting annoyed at this point and I'm shutting down.* It was just one step above the silent treatment. In the same way the van motor ticked as it cooled down, his wife's mood cooled down towards him. Erika was right. They rarely got out on a date night anymore. It was nice to have some quiet time together. Bill knew his wife and she had one weakness: spontaneity.

In the shadow of the school it was worth one more effort, "Hey, I have an idea." Bill said, "Let's go find a nice restaurant tucked away downtown, kind of expensive, not too expensive. Maybe we'll have a rude, snooty waiter with some exotic name that is annoyed that people like us are having dinner at his table."

"You already suggested we go have dinner somewhere else. I'm not too sure why your version of a wonderful night out involves tolerating poor customer service," replied Erika. "I'll take you up on this offer of yours after Christmas minus the rude wait staff. I want to go and have a nice evening. I would like to see where you went to school and meet some of your old friends. More important to me, I'm proud of you. I love the man you are. I couldn't ask for a better husband, father or provider. I know you're down because of how hard it's been getting hours in at work. We've always been provided for and have never been without."

"I just thought the rude waiter would add to a swank dining experience complete with the full cast of little forks and spoons. It'd be a nice change from ordering our dinner from a menu that just hangs off a wall behind some cashier. You know, ordering our dinner-by-numbers. I'll take a number seven please no mayo or onions."

On the surface it seemed like the reluctance to attend the reunion was almost childish or mildly selfish. It was going to be awkward to sit down and try to exchange witty dinner conversations about only a few notable experiences in his life. Not a lot has happened over the last twenty years. It was a safe estimate to believe by the time he had finished his first dinner roll, he would have shared his full life's experiences.

"Please pass a roll. Let's see I graduated, I got a job, I met Erika, purchased a home, and we have three children. Work is really slow. The roll was great you should try one."

What really worried him were the real issues pressing Bill making him want to leave and not set foot in that building. The distant memories and nightmares lurked deep in the recesses of Bill's mind. These memories were like ravenous animals only coming out at night when they sensed prey looking to devour a helpless soul wandering too close. These memories needed to stay in the dark, shadowy caves they had called home for over twenty years. The last thing Bill wanted to do was to stroll down memory lane next to these caves.

An expensive luxury sedan pulled up from behind them. The cars headlights lights went dark, and he heard the sound of a door opening and closing followed by muffled voices as a couple headed towards the school. An electronic chirp was activated letting the world know that an expensive car was parked there.

"Did you recognize them?"

Looking at the couple, all he saw was their shadow "No, I can't say I do. It's too dark. This is exactly what I'm talking about. Why spend an evening with people I don't know or pretend to know?"

"It's called a reunion, and I'm starting to get cold. Can we go in, please?"

"Two hours and we're done ok?"

"No, Sunshine. A minimum of three hours and at least one, maybe two, dances with me. The menu looked wonderful. Besides, they have pie for dessert and you like pie."

Grabbing his coat and climbing out of the van into the cold night air, he waited for Erika as she walked around to the front

"Watch your step in case there's black ice; please." as she

carefully stepped around to the front. Extending his arm out to her, she smiled.

"Ready? Love you. It will be fun; I promise."

"Famous last words, I love you to."

Gingerly walking through the parking lot, Bill could not help notice that a few of the cars cost almost as much as his house did. Some of his classmates seemed to have done well for themselves since graduation.

"I should've rented a car for us tonight , we could've driven in style instead of driving the old soccer mom wagon."

"You really need to stop this. Who cares what we drive? I don't and the kids don't. Is it out of your system yet? Are you ready for a good night?"

Reaching not only the door to the school, he also was reaching the threshold of Erika's patience. Not wanting to spend the rest of the night on the couch, it would be wise to let it go. A few hours with some strangers in a few awkward conversations would not compare with the wrath he would get from his wife for ruining her night out. She had looked forward to this since they ordered the tickets a few months back.

"Ok, I'm thinking I'm finished. We'll have a good time tonight."

"That's the spirit. One more time, I love you." Erika gave Bill a

kiss on the cheek as he opened the front door.

CHAPTER TWO

The first assailed sense was the sense of smell. A heavy strong odor of fresh paint filled his nose. Couldn't they have waited to paint the lockers till after this reunion? They were always painting these lockers; yet, Erika did not seem to react to the heavy chemical odor. As they walked along the corridors having the smell of fresh paint in his nose, Bill noticed the paint on the lockers was old, worn, scratched and marked over. Walking with the other reunion attendees, no one seemed to respond to the smell of fresh paint.

At the time when the class of 1988 attended Park City the acting principal was obsessed with freshly painted lockers. Much like a county road crew may tear up county roads and drop fresh asphalt with seemingly randomness draining a state coffer and irritate commuters, the lockers were painted with the same fashion. There were always lockers to paint somewhere.

The smell of painted lockers worked like a tuner dial on his conscious mind working to pick up a distant radio station. At first the radio broadcast was distant, weak and broken. With each step going deeper into the school the signal being transmitted grew in strength becoming ever more constant and closer at hand. The sight of the lockers, front offices, class rooms and hallways stood exactly as he remembered them twenty years ago. A small line was forming to check in as people embraced and shook hands.

Looking around the corridors it would not surprise Bill if at any minute a teacher would step out into the hallway and reprimand them for loitering in the hallways. The signal grew in clarity as if from a far-away place and time.

The sounds of lockers were being opened and slammed shut. The sounds of a rushing bustle carried up from somewhere deep in the darkened corridors. From somewhere a body of students rushed trying to get to classes in session twenty years ago. The din of the rush carried up the corridor. Growing closer, the sounds of hundreds of people carried through the corridors. Emerging out of the dark was the student body of Park City High School. They rushed past Bill, Erika and the other reunion attendees. Neither the students nor the adults were aware of one another. Bill stood giving every impression of a man who had just seen a ghost.

A terrible headache was gaining a foothold and it was too early to take more aspirin after the episode in his bedroom an hour ago. Bill was not suffering from some mild social anxiety while in the line to check in with the other alumni of Park City High. The corridors were teaming with ghost of themselves from twenty years ago. The quiet school had turned into a hub of ghost-like memories all around where he stood. It was his own private experience and left him feeling like he had just stepped off a merry go around. Bill wish he could return to the safety and comfort of his home and leave these ghost like memories in those corridors.

Erika whispered in his ear, "Do you recognize anyone? This is so much fun! I'm glad we came."

The signal was lost and the sharp images faded away; even the smell of fresh paint slipped from his nose. For the moment the ghost who had walked among Erika and him returned from where they came from. Calm and order returned, and the only people standing in the corridor once again were the middle-aged people he had walked in with a few minutes ago.

CHAPTER THREE

It was their turn to check in and he saw his name tag it read "William Cooper."

An energetic volunteer looked up and smiled "Hi… let me see. Billy, here is your name tag William Cooper."

"Yeah, it's just Bill now" Bill replied

Trying to not look to obvious a quick glance of her name tag read "Dianna Perkins"

"Hi Dianna, how have you been?"

"Been great Billy, err sorry Bill. Glad you guys could make it."

Nope no recollection of who Dianna was. Taking his name tag he felt a vicious jab to his side.

"Oh I'm sorry Dianna this. This is my wife Erika"

"Hi Erika, welcome to our reunion. I hope you and Bill have a wonderful night tonight taking that stroll down memory lane." Smiling at Dianna, he clipped his name tag to his lapel.

Dianna, in a most enthusiastic voice, "If you would take this form, we're having some door prizes at the end of the night. Also, were going to take up a donation to help finance a granite memorial in honor of any alumni who have lost their life serving our country. We're going to put it in the courtyard."

"That sounds like a great idea. I'll get this filled out, and see what I can do to help with the memorial."

"Super! Have a great time tonight."

Erika smiled at her and said, "Thanks."

Maneuvering through the lobby around some familiar and some not so familiar people, many of them wore name tags similar to Bill. Glancing down the corridors belonging to his classes for a season, the dim lighting of the corridors slowly rolled back, and the lights from the ceilings illuminated the student body again as they made their way to their classes. The halls reverberated with their voices. Conversations seemed to be alive with topics ranging from class work to upcoming plans for after school. Bill stood in the middle of them as they passed him without ever giving him a second glance.

As the hustle and bustle of the day went on around him, he recognized familiar banners hanging in the corridor. It had been a close season for their varsity basketball team that year. Several of the schools in their district were fighting for a place in the 1986 state championship high school basketball playoffs. Park City was favored to win a spot and the school was pulsed with school pride that day.

Though Erika was walking next to him, she may as well have been on the moon. She was unaware of the sea of students teaming through the corridors many times walking right between the two of them. Bill had been in a stable marriage for seventeen years, and the father of three small children; yet, at this moment he was overwhelmed with a sense of isolation. Hidden within the mass of students a silent lone figure met his gaze, a face peered back at him from within the humanity passing bye. A face he had not seen in twenty years. There in the halls stood Billy. The boy's eyes were hollow and emanated no life from within. Despite life swirling around Billy he was oblivious to it because of a choice made the night before one with forever consequences.

From the distant lunar surface, a voice broke the trance Bill was in, "Hey handsome. Are you coming? Looks like the gyms this way or did you forget?"

"No, I'm sorry. It would seem memory lane has turned into an expressway and we're standing in the middle of it."

"I'm sorry. I thought this would be fun. We won't stay to long, ok?"

"No, I'm fine. Let's go find our seats."

They found their way into the gymnasium and took their seats.

"I'd like a glass of wine; do you want one?" Erika asked as she sat down and pulled her chair in.

"No I'm fine. I think I'll just have a club soda. You go ahead and enjoy one for the both of us."

"Are you sure? It's your reunion."

"No, really I'm fine." After feeling like he had been kidnapped from this reality the last thing he wanted was something possibly altering his perception even more. "I'm good, Erika. You enjoy."

Going to the open bar and finding his place at the back of the line he took in some of the hastily thrown up decorations. That morning, this had been a functioning gymnasium. Now, plastered all over the gym, was an assortment of streamers mixed with a half dozen slow revolving disco balls. The impersonal white glow of floodlights had been replaced with a softer lighting trying to hide the high school gymnasium and more like a ballroom dressed up for the prom like so many times over the years. The DJ worked the crowd skillfully luring a few souls out onto the empty dance floor. Small groups instinctively stood with their old familiar cliques. Though time may have changed their bodies, it had not changed the social strata laid out twenty years ago.

Like a morning fog being burned away with the rising sun, the soft, dark atmosphere drew away from the presence of an afternoon sun shining down from the windows high above the maple floor. Tables, chairs and the enthusiastic DJ much like the soft lighting were hidden by the afternoon sun. The sunlight revealed bleachers full of a student body. The school was holding an afternoon spirit rally; they were going to enjoy the home team advantage that night. It was held at the end of the day and their voices echoed off the wooded floor. Not wanting to look, Bill lowered his head because he knew where he sat on that day. From his place in line, distant muffled voices of adults joked how a certain history teacher wore the same suit several times a week. They debated its color and fabric. From where Bill stood and what he could see about the teacher in question, they were all wrong. Though the teacher passed away many years ago, Bill could walk across the gym floor and shake his hand. Leaving his place in line he stumbled through the crowd as cheerleaders did cartwheels or middle aged people dressed in evening gowns and suits held cocktails. The cheerleaders were oblivious to the much older versions of themselves sitting near them talking about how their children were honor roll students at junior high schools. Finding the bleacher he had occupied that day, he turned and watched as the Park City student body cheered for their mascot. A cascade of boos rained down at the sight of their opponents makes-shift mascot running out onto the gym floor. A DJ from a distant place worked a different crowd. The cheer squad worked the student body in a fevered pitch of school spirit and cheer. It seemed an infectious wave of spirit swept through the bleachers impacting all but one student. Standing at the foot of his assigned bleacher, Bill recognized the boy from the hallway. Billy approached and took his seat.

The final minutes of that school day started to tick away. The students would be released from the pep rally and would briefly return to their classes. From there, the school would be dismissed for the weekend. Though he stood in front of the bleachers he could feel himself seated, wedged in tight with other students. Looking up at the clock on the wall, time weighed heavily on his heart. How much time was left in the rally, class or bus ride home?

As the spectacle of the rally went on, thoughts of egg shells filled his mind: a lifetime of walking them. Years of living in the home of an angry man, on some days he looked for reasons to take his rage out on Billy. Having never spent a day in a war zone, he reasoned to guess there may be some similarities with his life and a war zone.

Soldiers who lived their lives on the front line lived with the understanding at any given moment they could suffer harm or death without warning. Days, weeks or years were spent trying to live life in that state, always living life with their guard up, never wanting to lay it down had to be an exhausting way to live. Surely years of that would take its toll on a human soul.

Living with a person who had the ability to injure without warning had made Billy live his life with his guard up. Never knowing what hour or day he may be harmed had drained his soul of life. He was exhausted.

His father's parenting philosophy was a simple concept "I'll either break you or make you Billy." There was nowhere to go for help outside of the home. If his father found out he had sought assistance, it may insight a vicious backlash. No one seemed to notice that Billy rarely practiced good hygiene. While his peers wouldn't dare leave the house without so much of a hair out of place unless of course it was by design, Billy didn't have the energy for such a care or worry.

The clock continued to wind down. Six months prior to this day, he had decided to take his life. It would be better to end things on his terms than having to stomach being called a "fucking loser" again by his father. That previous summer, Billy attempted some dry runs trying to work up the nerve to actually cross the threshold separating life and death. A stern hand inside of him held Billy back never allowing him to take that final step.

The days, weeks and months passed and each day he got off the bus he wanted to fall to his knees in the street and scream for someone to throw him a lifeline. Confined to an invisible prison, a prison people outside of his home would never see, Billy thought surely few, if any, of his peer's parents threatened to break their teeth out because of failing grades. The stress and fear had destroyed what little of concentration he had left. The preoccupation of ending his life made seeing beyond the next twelve months impossible. Alone in his world, he watched with a detached curiosity wandering how the game would be decided that night.

As the team captains made statements to further fan the flames of hype, Billy enjoyed a private victory. Never again would he be dragged out of the bed long after he had gone to bed to be yelled at until the early morning hours. After one of those nights, it was difficult to go back to sleep and try and get up and go to school. Many times it was not the grades making his father blow into a rage but the teacher's comments that set him off in ranting violent rages.

"Billy is so capable. He simply does not apply himself."

Billy thought if only these teachers were not so open with their comments his father hurt him less. On some occasions those sarcastic "helpful" remarks would be all it took for Billy to receive a swollen lip from his father's hand. Sometimes he would go easy on Billy and just throw something at him; whatever was close at hand. Maybe a plate of food, on one occasion he picked up a chainsaw and swung it at him. He missed Billy and hit his truck instead causing a large scratch. This brought about a cascade of verbal abuse as though it had been Billy's fault for not taking the blow of the saw. His aim was always bad; the alcohol in his blood helped with that.

Other nights he would brew silently over his glass of whiskey and glare at him. Sometimes he would not hit but without warning leap from his chair with a balled fist ready to punch but at the very last minute stop. Billy could not shake off the feeling his legs were quivering at the sight of his larger father coming at him with a balled fist. Billy lived his life on egg shells never knowing if this day or the next day would be good or bad. What would set the man off: a chore not completed to his satisfaction or a missed homework assignment?

Humiliation was one his father's favored parenting philosophies. He thought one way to help his son to remember homework was to send him to school with his own report card system. It required each day for his son go to the front of the class at the end of periods and have teachers initial off a form letter there had been no work to take home. His father's note apologized that his son was unable to manage his own homework. His classmates would snicker at him and ask to see the form letter or open his notebook while he was away from his desk and read the form letter out loud to the class. Pleading with his father to stop with the signed form letters it was always, "start managing your own work and I'll stop. You'll never amount to anything in life Billy. You're just one notch above a loser, just a tad over one, Billy."

By far the most dreaded of all 'disciplines' was the brown steel chair. This consisted of sitting confined in his room for days on end wasting away in a brown steel chair. When he had been sentenced to time in the chair, days would consist of long hours slowly wasting away from the time he got off the school bus until nine at night. On weekends: from the time he got up until the time he went to bed. He longed for bedtime to get out of that chair. Should a school holiday fall on days he had been sentenced to time in the chair his father treated it like a weekend schedule: all day with no break other than a meal or respite to the bathroom, alone in his bedroom with nothing to look at but bare walls and a window. The only view from the window was a long, empty, barren field. On the far side of the field stood a tangled woods mixed with rotten logs, honey suckle bushes, briars and an occasional poison ivy vine. While at the desk, he was only permitted to do homework or sit and stare at the green desk blotter sitting across the desk. The casual trip to the bathroom seemed like going he was going on a vacation. Any diversion to get out of that steel chair.

The days dragged on. One afternoon Billy made a wonderful

discovery, in a bottom desk drawer was a treasure box. He was in total awe and wonder holding the small plastic box in his hand. How had this treasure been overlooked? Surely his father had not seen this. If he had, it would have been removed in short order. How many days, weeks or months had this wonderful box been within his grasp just ready to be discovered? With care he opened the plastic lid and inside was close to five hundred map pins. The pin tops were in a variety colors: red, black, blue, green, red, and white. To Billy the tops were not just colored plastic tops. They were soldiers, archers, knights and kings, mighty armies ready to conquer kingdoms and set out on great adventures. What a find this was! With care, Billy set the pins out on the desk and organized them by color. Alliances were made between the different colors. At the bottom of the box were several gold colored thumbtacks. These made the perfect kings and queens for his imaginary armies. The hours past as he made up stories using the map pins. Kingdoms rose and fell during those days.

CHAPTER FOUR

It was Bill's turn to collect his drinks. He told the bartender what he wanted, "White wine and a club soda with lime please."

The bartender poured Bill and Erika's drink. He tossed a five into the tip jar and waded back through his classmates to his seat next to Erika. The warmth of her eyes and gentle caress of her hand across his hand served as a reminder his life was there with her, not in a steel chair pushing push pens across a desk blotter.

Their table was filling up with former classmates accompanied by their invited guest. The table buzzed with light conversation and shared laughs. Wonderful memories were passed around as his peers regaled one another with their different life's accomplishments: places they had gone, higher educated, businesses owned. A distant voice haunted his thoughts. Looking down at the calluses on his hands, skin

worn raw from carrying shingles high up a ladder, thoughts of a broken

down van and a busted hairdryer, the voice haunting him was right.

This voice said he was "just one notch above a loser; a fuck up; never

amounting to anything." Taking a sip of water listening to his beautiful

wife make friends with his peers, he smiled. The voice was not totally

right; she had married him. She had shared her life with his; she was

the mother of his three children. It was enough to silence the ugly voice

trying to pile on the sense of wasted life. Trying to pry open the door to

his heart and mind. Erika was a beautiful intelligent woman and she

married him. He couldn't be all that bad.

 A hand suddenly landed on his shoulder from behind, and the

smell of alcohol laced through his nose. Bill turned to see an old friend;

one of the few he had considered to be a friend. They both had been

awkward in school and misery loved company. They had not spoken

since high school.

 "Mark, wow it's good to see you."

 "Hey, Billy, I thought that was you. You look great. Do you

work out or something? How do you stay so fit looking?"

"I work outside a lot. You look great also. How have you been?"

"Good, I've been busy. I manage people's money for a living. I'm a financial advisor. Do you think about your future? How's your portfolio performing? Let me give you my card and just give me a call. We'll work out a plan right for you. Or hell, we'll just sit have a beer and catch up. Hey, who's this with you?"

"Sure, that sounds good. This is my wife Erika. We've been married seventeen years and have three children."

Erika turned, smiled and extended her hand.

"Erika this is my childhood friend, Mark. I used to ride my bike to his house. On some weekends, we'd just hang out and stuff."

Mark put his arm around Bill's neck and pulled his old friend tight, "Yeah Erika, your husband and I really used to be a team. We were a couple of tough guys really mixed it up with some of the tough kids and we really had the ladies chasing after us."

"We're not talking about the same man. I think you have the wrong table."

"Yeah, your husband was a good kid. We spent a lot of time riding our bikes. Remember how we used to pretend those bikes were old World War I fighter planes and we'd go out on morning patrols over France during the war? Just pretend we were flying. Two old buddies all day on bikes," Mark paused and took a sip of his drink. "When we *could* get together, you were a good friend and those are some of my best memories. Just two kids with nothing but blue sky and the fate of the free world on our shoulders."

Bill smiled, "How could I forget? We would probably bike a couple hundred miles those summers blazing a trail of glory and drinking gallons of your mother's lemonade."

Mark swirled his drink and looked down at it. "Those were simple days spending the afternoon shooting the Red Barron from the sky. Then, we would land and sit next to the old pond on the farm halfway between our houses and talk about girls and wonder where life would take us when we grew up. Well buddy, it's here. I hope life has been good to you."

"It's been ok, I can't complain. We have our health." Bill

offered.

"Well it's better than nothing. I'll drink to your health my old wingman." Mark toasted his old friend.

Bill changed the subject to get the topic off of him, "So Mark how about you, married? Do you have any children of your own?"

Mark thoughtfully "No brother, not as lucky as you. I've tried twice and it's just not for me. That's my date over there." Mark pointed his little finger over at a very attractive woman who waved back at Mark. Mark leaned in and whispered "She's from the Ukraine and she's really into me. So for a few weeks it'll be fun then I'll just move on." Mark paused for a minute. "No kids. I would make a lousy father. I'm too busy with work."

"Oh, hey, let me show you mine."

Bill pulled from his wallet a few pictures that containing his life and joy. Only a few minutes had passed between the two men but it seemed not to long ago two boys would have spent an entire day together exploring dusty lanes around their homes. Miles would pass beneath their meandering bikes while their imaginations soared high above the clouds. They were pilots breathing in the cold crisp air on a morning patrol over the villages dotting the French countryside talking about girls and looking for an enemy to shoot from the sky. Two old friends: a twice married money investor with a date from the Ukraine and a happily married roofer the father of three children. Their dusty roads had long been paved over; no longer the scene of brutal dog fights high above the killing fields of France during "The Great War." The only testimony remaining to their friendship was a few memories and the lonely black top surfaces covered in salt and snow that night. Two friends shook hands one last time and shared a brief man-hug complete with a back slap and a goodbye.

Bill sat back down and missed his old friend. Watching him go sit next to that beautiful girl from the Ukraine, he wished one more time they could mount up their bikes, strike "contact!", taxi down the runway, and take off back into the sky and fly. Few things brought Bill any joy when he was growing up and spending time with his friend, Mark, was the one thing he always looked forward to. Twisting a napkin into a tight ball and rolling it in the palm of his hands, the conversations around him drifted away and seemed to matter very little. What mattered to Bill, his childhood friend and one particular Saturday when they were eleven years-old.

The weather promised to be one for the records. It was Friday after school and an early spring. The air was sweet with blossoms and fresh cut grass. With the warm weather in the forecast, it pointed to a great weekend for bike riding. The two friends were eleven years old and veteran aces having spent many hours in the cockpits of their biplane fighters. The fuselages of their planes were decorated with many kills and they were feared by their enemies. As the bus rumbled down the dusty lanes, Mark and Billy made their plains for the weekend.

"I'll meet you at the Baker Farm Pond at thirteen hundred hours sharp, ok Billy?"

"Thirteen Hundred Hours? Why not, oh, nine hundred hours? That's the time patrol usually starts." Billy protested.

Mark moaned "I can't my mom is taking me to buy shoes at the mall and a haircut but I can meet you after that."

"Ok, I'll meet you then," Billy agreed.

Deep down, the eleven year old Billy knew it was a pipe dream. He would never be allowed to meet his friend. It had been report card that day, and his grades were bad, again. His father usually did not take this very well and would probably restrict him to the chair for the weekend. He just wanted to enjoy the feeling he would be able to meet his friend. He would have to call Mark that evening and cancel their patrol.

There was one worrisome remark and it said, "Billy rarely turns in assigned homework." Billy's mind was always wandering far away and he had trouble concentrating. That night over dinner Billy slid his report card across the dinner to table to his father. Opening the envelope he looked over the grades, put the grades back into the envelope, sealed it shut and looked at him,

"All this semester you've had homework and you just never bothered to do any of it?"

"Yes, sir I have." Billy slowly replied.

"You've been lying to me all this time." His father said calmly as he returned the grades back into an envelope.

Billy sighed and any hope of spending Saturday with his friend was slipping through his grasp. "Yes sir."

"Yes, sir, what?"

"I've been lying to you." Billy felt it was not entirely true. He just forgot, could not get organized and had difficulty focusing. Sliding his chair out from under the kitchen table his father stood up, picked up the report cards and looked his son in the eyes "Tell you how I am going to deal with this. You have one of two choices. I will let you decide what your discipline should be. Your first choice is you sit in your chair at the kitchen table all weekend. It starts right now and will go all day tomorrow and all day Sunday. While you sit at this table you'll write all weekend 'I will not lie to my father, and I will do all my homework.' All weekend you will write that. The other choice is I take you out into the garage and beat you with the belt. Take the whipping and you're free to spend your weekend the way you want. The choice is yours. I'll be outside waiting for your answer, son." His father took his drink and walked outside to leave Billy alone to his thoughts.

CHAPTER FIVE

The sound of the screen door slammed shut as his father went outside. There was no way he wanted to sit in that steel chair. Feeling slightly more confident, he could salvage his weekend at the expense of a very painful back. The window was open and the sweet smell of spring wafted through the screened window. The brown heavy leather belt was no small matter. It was thick and heavy. The pain would last only a moment; the chair would last all weekend. Trying to muster his strength, Billy slid the chair out from under the table and walked towards the screen door. Reaching the door and putting his hands on it, he paused for a moment making sure this is what he wanted. Billy could see his bike against the garage. Patrol was at thirteen hundred hours tomorrow afternoon. Billy knew he was a highly decorated ace and no stranger to fear. He felt the chair for the weekend was the coward's way out; he wanted to spend time with his friend.

Pushing the screen door open, "Dad I will take the beating."

"Good son I'm proud of you. Let's go I'll make it quick."

The two of them headed out into the garage breathing the sweet spring air that was soon to be his. The sound of ice cubes clinked in his fathers after-dinner drink as they went into the garage. The door closed behind him. The sweet air was replaced with the smell of wood, gas and oil. It was a dark and dusty place. Having to assume the position with his back side exposed and from the corner of his eye, Billy watched as his father bent the belt in half and started to reach high above his head. Closing his eyes and turning his bare back to his father, Billy thought of tomorrow. The sound of the motor turning over, their two planes would taxi with the wind from the props blowing against their faces. The first blow came against his skin. The boys would stand up on their pedals and pedal as fast as they could, working to gain altitude. The engines would scream as they would try to break the laws of gravity looking to gain loft. Another blow bit though his skin. More power from the throttle and the two friends would be in the sky free from the ground. With a slow bank of the wings, they would circle the dirt lane with the smell of honeysuckle in their nose and the wind in their hair. Barely feeling the final blow, Billy was high in the air with his good friend Mark. Billy was free. .

His father told him to go inside and clean up. Never before had his father told him to clean up after he had taken the belt to him. Going inside the bathroom, he closed the door behind him and looked in the mirror. He now understood why his father told him to clean up. There was blood. The bathroom door opened and his father looked in and told him to tell no one about the blood or bruises. After he cleaned up Billy went outside and made his bike read for the next day. The bike chain was greased and tires pressure checked. He got some bungee cords together so he could strap his canteen, a lunch box and a box to carry some comic books. Saturday was going to be a great day. What happened in the garage was worth having the day free.

The next day just as the weather man promised, the weather was perfect, sunny, not a hint of humidity and low seventies. Billy went outside and got his bike ready to head out and meet Mark at the pond. The pond was several miles away halfway between his home and Mark's home. As he was getting ready to go back inside to make his lunch, the screen door opened, his father came out, and asked where he was going. Billy told his father the plans were to meet Mark at the pond near the farm and spend the day on their bikes.

A sickening realization swept over the eleven year old boy: his father had changed his mind. Billy would not be able to spend the weekend free and his father needed help around the property since there a lot of chores needed to be done that weekend. He wanted to till and expand the garden in the back yard. There would be a lot of rocks to be hand carried out of the garden, and that is where his father needed him that day and the next. Billy's father strolled past leaving Billy in stunned silence looking at the screen door where he was just about to go and fix his lunch for the day.

As Billy carried piles of rocks from the garden he thought of his friend he had stood up. His back was still raw after the time in the garage. Billy thought to himself he should have stayed in the chair. It would have been spared the belt beating. One by one the rock pile grew. Using his imagination in the same way the map pins came a live Billy looked up into the sky and enemy fighters dove out from in front of the sun on his friends "six". Billy would open the throttle and the engines of his biplane would roar to life as he dove in on the enemy fighters trying to protect his friend's tail. Then they would land, find a shade tree, and enjoy their lunch, share comics, and talk about girls. The rocks were not so heavy anymore.

Bill twisted his napkin in a tighter roll, and he really wanted some air. The restroom was not far away, and he needed to excuse himself to try to regain some of his composure. Bill slid his chair out and kissed Erika on the head; he needed a trip to the men's room. Quickly walking across the gym floor, he reached the other side and opened the door. Walking out into the hall it was quiet as the gym door closed with a heavy clunk. For a moment, the only sound he heard was the thumping from the DJ entertaining the alumni. Bill smiled at a few of his peers milling about in the hallway looking at old pictures in trophy cases.

Walking down the empty hallway instead of going to the men's room he searched for his old locker. It was good to get away from all of the stories flowing around the table about vacations abroad or how one peer recommended an "I" series sports sedan over the "L" class. Skiing at one destination had better powder than another spot. Business flourished. No one seemed to want to hear stories of just sitting in the yard on a warm day resting in a lawn chair with feet soaking in a small plastic pool enjoying the cool water on his feet while watching a four year old little girl splash around in the pool. Then Anna would soak his shirt because she insisted on hugging him after jumping out of the pool. There was no time for drying off when Anna was swept with the desire to hug Bill. Not exciting dinner conversation in the least. Bill's footsteps fell silently along the empty dark corridors as the sound of splashing water and the laughter of that blue-eyed, blonde sun-kissed little girl played in his ear.

Coming to the student common area, it had not changed in

twenty years. There was the bulletin board just like then. There was an announcement giving instructions on how to secure a seat on a charter bus for an away varsity basketball game next week.

The sound of his Anna playing in the pool on that warm day drifted away as the student common area was no longer dark or quiet. There was the sound of students tossing book bags into lockers from behind him. In a mad rush to start their weekend, students grabbed their coats and picked out books to take home for the weekend to do homework assignments due on Monday. Monday seemed like a world away; it was Friday afternoon and the school was ready to enjoy that night's game.

With the dark fading away and the sunlight shining through the windows, the dingy lockers looked shiny again and fresh paint filled his nose once more. Standing in the common area was probably why Bill had such an aversion to the smell of fresh paint. It always reminded him of this day. The smell nauseated him.

There was a dull roar from hundreds of different conversations all mingling at once. Bill found his locker among the rush of students heading out for the day. They did not see him as they passed him by. It was just a memory he told himself as he touched his locker. He and Mark had drifted away when they started high school. When the day came that airplanes were no longer important and conversations turned towards cars, Mark started to hang around older kids who drove cars.

They passed him in the hall. Billy longed for someone to invite him over to their home and watch a movie on a VCR or ask him if he would like to ride along and get pizza with them. Maybe they would check and see if he had ride for the game that night. Billy opened his locker one last time and carefully stacked his books one by one. There was a calm surrender in front of his locker. The time had wound down, the rally was over, the school day was finished and the only thing left was the bus ride home.

The days of sitting in a steel chair were over. The man would never pull him across the house by his ear, curse him or call him a loser. No longer would that man hurt him or would he live in fear of him. Billy's days of a silent prison were going to be over in a few hours.

Billy thought at the moment he pulled the trigger he would fly far away and high above the place supposedly called a home. He was going to bank above the clouds but not for pretend this time while pedaling a bike over a dirt lane. This time flying would be for real.

The halls started to thin out as the students carried themselves to their different busses. With the locker door standing open in his mind Bill remembered *the* moment when he decided to end his life. The moment occurred in the kitchen of their home on a Thursday evening the day before the big basketball game.

Billy's brother, Danny, had gotten an exceptionally bad report card very much out of the norm for him. Danny was better at school work than his older brother and was seven years younger than him. Billy stood in the kitchen with Danny and their mother, the three of them huddled over Danny's grades. Hidden in Billy's pockets were his grades; he had not shown them to her yet. Billy's stepmother asked to see Danny's report card first. Looking over her son's grades, she was showing a good deal of anxiety. She was not used to seeing these much lower grades from Danny. Billy could see she was truly afraid for her son, Danny.

With a heavy heart she said, "Danny your father is going to be furious over these."

At that point, Billy bit his lip out of fear for his brother. Billy could not stand to see his brother go through the things he had been through. Danny started to cry in fear because he had seen how his father treated his older brother and was afraid it would happen to him. Billy's step mother held her son, comforted him and gazed up at her step-son Billy hoping his grades were much worse so he would receive the brunt of what was coming when their father got home.

She made the comment that shook his being. It was a frantic remark made in haste but the truth hurt; "For your sake, I hope your grades are better than these because frankly I would not put it pass him to really hurt you. "

Billy's grades were far worse than Danny's. The three of them in the kitchen knew what storm was going to hit their home when he came home in a few minutes. He looked at his brother hiding his face in his mother's arms. Billy had reason to believe her. He knew he would be hurt badly that night. It had to stop. With his brother whimpering in his mother's arms, Billy calmly looked at his mother and said he did not have his grades yet. He would have them on Monday and they were some of the best grades he had ever earned. Surely this would calm his father down and he would ease up on his little brother. Billy had sealed his fate with that lie. It bought the two boy's time. His father would be in a good mood because his oldest son finally had some above average grades. Billy considered their father would shrug off Danny's poor grades as a fluke. If he showed the man these grades in his pocket he would warm up first on Danny and then he would let loose on him.

Over the years, Billy learned to listen for his father. The man owned a truck with oversized tires. The tires made a loud roar as they rolled over the asphalt. They could be heard a couple of miles from the house. Over the years he had learned to listen to the sound of those tires and pray to God the man was in a good mood. He would listen to the truck pull up in the driveway; the sound of gravel crunching beneath the wheels. He would hear the motor shut off, footsteps across the gravel and the familiar squeak of the screen door as he came into the house. There would be silence for anywhere from a few minutes to an hour. He would know in sixty minutes or less if it was a bad night or a good night. From outside came, the sound of the tires crunching across the gravel. He smiled at his step mom with all the fake confidence so she would believe him and that would help convince his father the lie was true.

The screen door opened and his father came in. With his report card stuffed in his pockets, his father asked what was wrong with Danny. Billy's stepmother explained to his father the boy had a fluke semester and his grades were below Danny's father's expectations. She felt Danny's grades would improve the next semester, and she promised to work with him. The man looked at Billy.

With a report card covered in red ink and a little brother with tear stained eyes he stood and looked up holding his father's eyes. "I did not get my grades. I will get them on Monday and I have been told by the teachers that they are my best for the year dad."

Billy's father tossed his coat on a chair and looked at their mother. "Well good, it'll be ok. Danny had an off- semester."

He walked to the front of the house leaving the three of them alone in the kitchen. The storm had passed. His brother would be ok; Billy realized he had burned his ship. There was no coming back from that moment. Billy would end it tomorrow in the woods behind their house with a rifle.

Billy basked that night in the peace that had come over the home. He shuddered to think what would have happened to him and his brother. Danny played and forgot the fear he had felt at being in their father's grasp. While Billy rested in his bed that night he thought of his father's words

"I'm either going to make you or break you, boy." His father had broken him.

Standing in front of his old locker much like he had done over twenty years ago Bill could remember thinking. "Will the gunshot hurt? Would it be over quickly? What will it be like to fly with the wind? What will the other kids say that Monday? Would they notice him being gone?"

The thought of flying with the wind made Billy relax and the peace of knowing he would not be in pain anymore gave him the strength to pull his parka out of the locker, and shut the door. Turning with conviction, Billy headed towards the bus to take him home.

Walking back to the gym to find Erika, Bill followed the same route towards the front of the school where the busses parked to take students home back then. As an adult Bill saw ghost-like teachers standing in the halls saying goodbye to the student body. Bill wanted to grab them and yell at them to stop Billy. How was it they did not see the boy was drowning? Bill knew they had no way of knowing Billy lived in a home where he had just been threatened his father would hurt him. They had no way of knowing. He sat locked in a steel chair for days on end. Bill stood and watched Billy walk towards the exit with no books in hands. Billy did not need to take anything home from school that day. Bill walked away from the student lockers. It was time to leave this place.

Finding his seat next to Erika, she was being herself. Free and full of life, she had blessed him by sharing her life with him. He had known love and patience because of her. Outside the wind blew and snow fell, but inside he basked in her company. No more did he lay awake afraid someone would come in his room and drag him outside into the night insisting he finish his chores in the rain. He would lay awake at night and listen to her sleep in peace. While the stories went on about how easy things seemed to be for everyone else, she and the kids had been the only thing beautiful in his life. Bill wished he could provide for her the way his peers seemed to provide. She did not need to worry her van may break down from beneath her at any minute.

"Are you ok?"

"Yeah I'm fine. I would like to leave in a couple of hours if that's ok."

"I ordered you the Roast Beef"

"Sounds good, you know me"

"Yes I do, I wish you would try some new things. I think you would like the fish if you tried it."

"Why do that and waste a meal I know I'm going to like for a chance on something I may not like? I guess if all they had was fish, I

would give that a try."

CHAPTER SIX

The food came. It was ok. Feeling relieved the entrees were being served meant Bill was in the home stretch as far as calling this night a wrap.

Erika leaned in and whispered in his ear, "You won't deny me a dance will you?"

"No I won't"

Sliding their chairs out and moving to the dance floor, a slow popular song from twenty years ago. Erika slid her arms around Bill's neck and pressed her warm body next to his. The familiar scent of her hair conditioner smelled like home. It was home, their home. She and the kids never had an inkling of what it felt like to live in fear of one you were supposed to trust and look to for protection. Feeling a stir in his heart at that thought, the madness had stopped with him on that day. There would no longer be boys cowering in fear at the sound of their father's footsteps across the threshold following that day.

Despite the peace and joy he felt from holding Erica as they enjoyed their first dance in years, he felt a tremendous sense of failure. Their life was a constant struggle for the basics. What did she see in him? He had barely graduated high school, struggled to keep a roof over her head. His peers would go back to their world of success, and he would go back to his world of carrying shingles up a ladder in the cold if he got any work that week.

The dimly lit gymnasium and its temporary disco balls hanging from the ceiling gave way to bright banners proclaiming "Park City Pride", "Lion Country", and " Park City Lions #1". The sun light pierced the darkness shrouding the windows high above the gym floor with a soft glow. As if the sunlight from a memory twenty years old had an expiration date for sparkle and just like sparkling cider that had gone flat, the sun appeared dull, flat and lacked any sort of radiance. Peering into the gymnasium, he watched with envy as the basketball team warmed up. Cheerleaders and the band all practiced their different routines all preparing for their spirit roles at that night's game. Many kids milled around on bleachers visiting with friends. They were smiling, laughing, and goofing off with one another. Billy wanted to sit down with them to be included in their circles. Did any of them feel like ice water was coursing through their body when they heard their father walk through the door like he did? Did they panic when they heard the sound of oversized truck tires roar over black top when he was a mile away from the house? It was not his place to know. This was his life. Billy turned and headed out of the school to board his bus.

Bill held Erika tight as they moved in rhythm to a slow retro hit from the 1980s. Erika's warm breathing in his ear was serving as a tether, anchoring him to the shores of the present. With that security around him, he ventured further into the torrent of memories threatening to sweep him away.

Boarding the noisy bus that afternoon, Billy hoped it would be possible to have a nap for the ride home.   On average, the bus ride lasted for an hour. The last thing he wanted to do was watch the miles slip by. Each mile that slipped by would test his resolve for the business of the day.

The bus let Billy off at his stop. At that hour of the day, the only ones at home were his grandfather and Danny. Many days during the week, their grandfather would be napping heavily when they got home from school. Walking through the door, he noticed his Grandfather was asleep in his usual spot in a worn reclining chair. He never stirred as Billy came through the door. Danny was fully engrossed in the TV enjoying his favorite cartoons and did not notice his older brother had just walked through the front door.

Going into his bedroom and closing the door quietly behind him, in haste, he went to his desk with the green blotter and removed a sheet of paper and pencil. Leaving some sort of note behind seemed appropriate. Staring at a blank sheet of paper he could think of nothing to say to his family. He scribbled an apology, a goodbye and brief obligatory "I love you." Billy felt like his mouth was full of dry crackers. He left the room went to the bathroom and turned on the bathroom sink. As water flowed from the bathroom faucet, an image gazing back at him caught his attention. Looking from the mirror stood a person with ashen skin, gaunt features and hollow eyes. A dead person was looking at Billy from within the bathroom vanity mirror; he watched as the dead person drank the water. Billy tossed the paper cup away and left the bathroom.

Going back into the foyer to get his coat, Danny and his grandfather still paid no attention to Billy. This allowed him to walk into his father's study where he kept his rifles. He opened the gun cabinet and pulled out his .22 caliber rifle. At the top of the cabinet sat boxes of bullets. Billy removed one .22 caliber hollow point and put the bullet in his pocket. Wrapping the rifle in his coat, he walked out of the study back to his room. Danny never looked up from his cartoons, and his grandfather continued to lightly snore.

Back in his room, he looked out the window across the field and knew he had to get to the woods over half a mile away without being caught. About a hundred yards into the woods ran a small creek. This creek would provide an ideal spot to finish this. It was isolated and offered a peaceful setting. It was also far enough away that the sound of the gunshot would cause little concern. It was late hunting season and not uncommon to hear rifle fire at this time of day. Running the length of the field and going into the woods was a rarely used old farm lane.

Neatly folding his note, he placed it in his pants pocket. Also remembering his report card, he folded those up neatly and placed them in his pants pocket. While putting on his coat and glancing towards the desk he had spent countless days laid the bible his grandmother gave him last summer. Billy put that into his coat pocket. It was too late at this point to gain any spiritual insights that may alter this course. However, some random passage may provide some form of comfort. He never looked at it before, but at the last minute, he decided to take it along. Sliding the window open and tossing the bible out, Billy slid the rifle out next. Pausing, looking around the room and whispering a goodbye to himself, he climbed out after the rifle. Landing softly, he turned and shut the window. Grabbing the rifle and the bible he headed out towards the woods.

There would be no turning back at this point. His heart raced wildly as he headed toward the barren farm lane and thought of his grandfather asleep in his reclining chair. There was a small chance he may surprise him and appear around a corner of the house. Once reaching the dirt lane he began a light jog in the direction of the woods on alert for any sounds indicating he was spotted running away from the house towards the woods with the rifle in his hands. Fear gave chase like an angry junkyard dog running down a group of trespassers, and the jog turned into a fevered run trying to stay one step ahead of it. As he ran towards the woods, he longed to be at school enjoying the night with the other kids. Running to set himself free forever from nights like the last night and never again to be threatened like that, he would no longer be afraid of someone he was supposed to love and trust.

The woman's words burned in his mind forever. "You better hope," her words echoed in his mind. The woods grew closer he answered her silently "or what?" Picking up the pace, he considered exactly "what" would mean to him. The woods provided a chance to be free from the "what" forever.

In no time Billy covered the length of that small dirt lane and reached what seemed like a safe place to cross back into the field. Certainly his grandfather hadn't noticed anything out of the ordinary. Placing the rifle on the other side of the fence he climbed over. Picking it back up Billy walked into the woods and out of sight. After walking about a hundred yards into the woods the small creek stood before him. Only ankle deep it lazily made its way through the woods. On the bank of the creek was a small milk crate he and Danny took to the creek last summer. They spent long lazy summer days trying to dam the creek up to make a swimming hole. Looking at his watch, it was a little after four o' clock in the afternoon. Normal time for his father to be home from work was five-thirty unless he got home early then it may be as early as five o' clock or quarter to five.

Picking up the crate and carrying it away from the creek Billy found what looked like a comfortable tree for him to rest his back against. Flipping the crate upside down he sat and placed his back against a small tree. Placing the rifle across his legs he allowed himself a few moments to just sit and watch his breath float up into the sky.

Other than the sound of an occasional breeze rustling dead leaves and the soft flow of water coming from the creek to his left, it was very peaceful. The woods were growing dark as the sun started to sink behind a distant ridgeline. Shadows grew across the forest floor acting as a steady reminder: time was passing. Despite the cold January air he started to have the sensation he was sweating heavily. He was only sitting still on the crate, but his breathing was growing rapid and shallow.

The sweat started to dry from his brow and he felt a chill down to his bones. A hat and a pair of gloves would have been a welcome relief as he sat still. He never stopped to consider just how long he may sit in the woods waiting to do this. If he thought it would have taken this long he would have thought to take gloves and a hat. He just never really thought he would be sitting there for very long.

Removing his Bible from the coat pocket, he flipped through some of its pages. His eyes tried to read some of the passages. It felt like they would not cooperate with him. The words were blurry and he struggled to comprehend the meaning from the passages. With his back against the tree and the rifle across his legs, Billy turned the pages of the book looking for some passage that may comfort his heart and bring peace to his mind. All Billy saw was black print on a white page.

Alone in the woods, the clock stopped and the trees stood in silent testimony to his final moments. Tossing the bible to the ground as chaos swept over his mind like an ocean sweeping over a sea wall during an intense storm, his will to live alerted his conscious mind this was no fleeting fantasy being entertained. Billy meant to end his life right here and now while sitting in front of this small tree not far from the small creek. The desire to live began a life and death struggle to regain control and put an end to this notion before it was too late.

The roar of the struggle inside him was deafening. Feeling like a prayer to God may quiet the noise down in his head. Billy closed his eyes and lowered his head. For the first time in his life he cried out to God. Wishing he knew a long worded, well thought- out- prayer much like a preacher may offer up on a Sunday morning, Billy tried to think of something to say but nothing came to mind. Feeling even more frustrated he tried to focus on just one request he could ask of God. Something, anything, nothing too complicated. The only request coming from Billy's mouth at the moment in time was a one simple sentence prayer, "Would you send an angel to save me from this moment? I'm lost and need your help."

Worried he hadn't said enough and was afraid God would not listen or answer this prayer. Billy squeezed his eyes closed in a reverent manner. Surely this would convey to God his sincerity. Whispering "amen" and slowly opening his eyes, Billy looked around hoping to see God had answered this prayer and dispatched an angel to pull him back from the edge of this abyss. Much to his disappointment, God had not answered him. The woods remained empty and quiet. No one was coming to help. Billy lowered his head and looked at the rifle lying across his legs and felt the bullet in his pants pocket.

The stress and anxiety wore heavily on his mind and he nodded quietly off to sleep. The chill of the air caused him to stir realizing he had lost track of time. He glanced at his watch. It was a few minutes before five o' clock. His head absolutely throbbed and his mouth felt parched. The chill, dry mouth and headache all added to the misery of just sitting there trying to find the resolve to push the trigger.

The nap did quiet the roar within his mind, and it seemed for the moment, Billy's mind had restored order and the will to live prevailed. As if he were locked in a deadly game of chicken, he blinked. The will to live was stronger than the desire to end his life in those woods, "I can't do this."

Jumping up and trying to shake off the pens and needles torturing his feet, he felt a tremendous sense of relief he had not gone through with shooting himself. Billy bent down, picked up the rifle and the discarded bible. He turned and started to walk back home, alive. The leaves and fallen branches crunched under his foot as he walked. That feeling of relief was draining away like someone had pulled a plug. There was something he had forgotten. After a few dozen paces he paused with an agonizing groan, his father had given him a very long list of chores to be done that night. These chores were supposed to be done before he got home from work that evening, and he would be home in about half an hour. Also, there was still the matter he needed to face up to the man for some of the worst grades ever put to paper. To add to the top of what was becoming a fast growing heap of trouble, he would still have to answer up to the lie he had sold them last night. This is what an animal must feel like when they step in a snare and are trapped; fear and panic set in. If he was in trouble last night then this was much, much worse.

Memories of standing in the garage with the belt opening the skin on his back paled in comparison to what Billy would go through with his father that night. He was more afraid to live like this than to die by his own hand. Like an exhausted swimmer caught in a rip current being carried away from the shore unable to take another stroke, despair carried him back to the crate. Going down under the water for the last time he slowly sank down on the crate and laid the rifle across his legs.

Well this is it. Billy opened the action to the rifle, pulled the bullet out of his pants pocket dropped the bullet in the chamber and shut the action closed. Billy turned the safety off and sat the rifle between his legs. Billy placed the muzzle in the center of his chest just to the left of his breastbone with the muzzle resting against the bone. Watching the breath from his lungs float up and away he hoped his soul would do the same. Feeling the muzzle against his chest he hoped this would not hurt, but if it did, let it be over fast. Though the small caliber rifle was a light rifle, it seemed to weigh a hundred pounds against his chest. The black empty void of the muzzle stood at ready for him to press down against the trigger.

Once again looking back up at the clouds he focused on the point where tree tops ended and the sky met. Reaching down the length of the rifle and touching the trigger, Billy kept his eyes up and focused on the focal point. Listening to the sound of nature and with eyes up, he paused one more second and depressed the trigger.

The rifle fired. Bill did not recall the .22 caliber being so loud, it made a dreadful roar as it exploded around him and through him. A white flash filled his eyes as the roar of the blast carried through the woods with a lasting roll. While the smell of bitter gunpowder filled his nose, the phrase "Oh Jesus!" blasted out of him.

Feeling like a world class heavy weight boxer had just taken a red hot poker out of a bed of glowing embers, he plunged that glowing poker deep inside of his chest. The blast drove him up and back. With his feet failing, Billy collapsed to the ground like a heavy over- stuffed sack.

Gradually the ringing in his ears subsided replaced by the sound of an occasional breeze moving through the woods. Rolling over onto his back he was surprised that he was still alive. Surely the bullet had hit the heart. Billy had put the muzzle in the center of his chest. Wanting to survey the damage that inflicted by the shot yet afraid to see how bad it was, he used the corner of one eye to look down fully expecting to see a large hole where an intact chest used to be just moments ago. The quick glanced revealed his chest did not have a cavernous hole. Feeling slightly more confident, he gingerly raised his head up off the ground and looked down at his feet. The only thing indicating anything was out of the ordinary there was a small tear in his coat no larger than a pencil eraser.

It was a dreadful moment when he started to feel warm creamy soup being poured down his shirt and coat. A heavy sweet aroma wafted up from the coat and filled his nose. Alarmed, he felt a crushing sensation starting to bear down on him after each breath he took. If he did not know any better, he believed he was drowning to death on dry ground. A vicious cycle was beginning, Billy wanted to sit up and allow gravity help him breathe. However, moving meant breathing faster, and each breath seemed to make the pressure worse. Laying still on the ground and trying to breathe softly required less effort; however, just laying still on his back made him feel like he was forced under water.

After hearing the shot from that rifle just moments ago he was relieved to hear the sounds of nature once again. The sound of the rifle shot was a sound he would want to forget forever. Unsure of just how much time had passed, he was overcome with a bitter sense of remorse for pushing the trigger. It was too late for remorse; what had been done was done. There was no way to bring that bullet back. Raising his head back up once more he was frightened to see so much blood starting to soak through the coat. Shadows from the trees and bushes grew with the passing of each moment trying to cover him forever.

As Billy's body laid on the ground and the shock of knowing he had just been shot wore off, the quiet sounds of nature was replaced with the sounds of his own tortured breathing in his ears. A still quiet voice reached out to him from somewhere close. The spoken words were as noticeable as a soft breeze on a hot, stifling summer day. Despite the fear gripping his tortured mind, it reassured and settled Billy.

This was not the sounds of his thoughts. The sounds of his thoughts were familiar to him. Though it was a whisper it could have carried over the chaos of a thousand other voices. It was not only a voice but a presence. Though Billy could not see who it was who spoke to him he knew there was something there with him, and it was grasping him tight and keeping him from falling over the black void rushing up to take him forever. This presence was also familiar like it had been with him before. A busy street corner and a small boy left to cross alone. A small foot reaches out to cross without a care and an invisible hedge slows the boy long enough to pause for another glance as a bus roars past. This time it revealed itself to Billy in spoken words.

It asked one simple thing of him:

"Name a reason to live"

Instinctively he knew he needed to answer the question. Even though he could not see whatever spoke to him, he did feel like it patiently waited for his answer. Looking up once again where the sky and trees met, he tried to push up against the agonizing sense of going back under the water. Only one thing came to mind; he was not able to bear up under this for much longer.

Then in the distance, Billy heard what sounded like familiar voices; voices of small children playing as clear to him as if he were near a playground and not in the woods. There were several different voices coming from somewhere near the creek. He was at home with them for there was a distinct familiarity to them. It was impossible. He knew a few minutes ago he was alone in the woods. In a short manner of time, the once quiet woods had been replaced by the sound of a distant whisper and what sounded like children playing just out of sight. His heart leapt for joy as the sounds of their life resonated within him. Surely he had heard them from somewhere in the past. This must have been a memory from some children he had heard from somewhere. Yet

his heart leapt for joy and it testified to his mind, indeed these voices

held his heart captive. No audio memory from obscure children would

cause his spirit to soar as if he had just lived a lifetime of joy in only a

few brief moments. Despite the crushing sensation of water pouring

into his lungs, Billy tried to picture their faces. Their sounds seemed to

have all the warmth of being at home. Not the home he had just ran

away from, but a home ahead of him further up his road of life.

Picturing a front door swinging open to welcome him home he stepped

through. Billy was greeted by shrieks of joy as these little voices cried

out for their daddy. His mind acted as if this was already a part of an

established daily routine. These children rushed him and leapt into his

arms. They were so eager to embrace him and welcome him home.

He wanted to sit down, look at their cut out creations already

hanging on a refrigerator door. Billy wanted to teach them how to

skillfully eat ice cream cones on hot summer days so they did not waste

too much of it. Though Billy was not a father he felt the love a father

may feel for his children he wanted to get up off the ground and go see the children just out of sight. Never before this moment had Billy entertained such desires. At this point in Billy's life his hearts treasure was to see the warm sunshine on those children's faces. Billy's head felt heavy as he rolled it over hoping to catch a fleeting glance wanting to see who brought him so much joy in his life's final moments. Though Billy's wilted body laid alone in the woods, his spirit was not alone.

Strength swelled back into his limp legs and arms while anger burned deep in him. Billy wanted to share his life with those children; he longed to be their father. There was a reason to live and he had an answer to offer up to the voice that had broken the silence and called out to him. No longer afraid of his father or what he may or may not do to him; he had fallen in love with those children. The love and life he longed to share with them was more powerful than any fear he may feel. That man could take him back out to the garage and whip him again and again or make him sit in that steel chair until his legs grew numb. It did not matter, he wanted to live and enjoy the simple joys with them: having ice cream cones with little ones who looked up to him and called him daddy. With what felt like the weight of a fully grown man standing on his chest, Billy let out such a cry that there would be no mistaking he wanted to live. Not only did he just want to live he wanted to live and experience the joy of being a father in the distant future.

"I want to be a dad," be it a whimper, a shout or a moan the presence holding Billy, spoke again and with that it started to lead him out of the woods that afternoon.

"That is a good reason. Crawl now"

The sound of the children playing and living drifted away from his ear but never from his memory. With a new hope and a will to live regardless of what anyone or anything would ever hand him, he had a date with his children at some point ahead of him. Rolling over and getting up on his knees, dizziness swept over him as he struggled to his feet. The sensation of drowning made standing very difficult but there was no time. He had to get to his feet and move now. He tried to steady his feet. He would've had better luck trying to move across the deck of a pitching boat at sea. It was going to be a long walk back through the woods, over uneven ground, around trees and through bushes. He would still have to cover the half mile or so across the field to get to the house where someone could call an ambulance. Pushing aside the feeling he might as well be trying to walk to the moon and with no other choice but to trust his feet and legs to get him there, he lowered his shoulders and began to crash his way through the woods.

Without warning one leg gave out and Billy pitched forward landing hard on the ground. There was no time to lay there and just take in what had happened, he needed to stand back up. Billy used a tree to help climb back up to his feet and continued to stumble through the woods. His legs and feet no longer felt like they were his and would not cooperate so he moved with the precision of a person moving in the dark in an unfamiliar environment. The will to live had regained control of his mind and was pulling out all of the stops as he tried to push through the woods.

The ground once again fell out from under his feet without warning, pitching forward and without the aid of his arms to break his fall Billy fell with another heavy blow. From somewhere in the fog of his mind, Billy could tell he had just fallen. Doubting he had made it very far and frightened he had so much ground to cover, he wept inside at the very realization he was not going to make in time. Lying on the ground once again it felt like a heavy man was standing on his back trying to drive his spine through his chest into the ground and he was trying to breathe against the tide of that pressure. In the stillness of his spirit, he whispered to the voice who spoke to him, he was trying to get out of the woods to find help. He considered he was not going to hold one of those precious children and he was going to die today.

The spirit speaking to Billy had not given up. It was still there with him and with more authority this time it seemed to yell through the haze of Billy's thoughts what it wanted him to do: "Crawl!"

It was telling Billy how to maneuver out of the woods. Each tree, log, and any sharp rocks protruding from the ground all stood as an obstacle to be traversed. As the ground pitched and heaved, a wall of briars could entangle him and hold him forever in those woods. Gasping to his protector who remained close to him he heaved, "Ok."

Lying prone on his stomach, he dug his feet into the ground and pushed while he pulled with his arms using all the strength he could summon while the lungs continued to labor against the tide of atmosphere and blood caused by the bullet to the chest. Lying still on the ground back at the crate had consumed so much energy, moving for his life through the woods seemed unbearable. While suffocating and growing weaker by the moment, he felt like he was moving with force across the forest ground.

While his mind swam in a murky haze, he had the faint realization he was bouncing along the ground like a limp rag doll. While detached and no longer a participant to the drama unfolding around him, his body moved forcefully through the woods while his face dragged over rocks and other debris. Privately, when he shared the events of the day with a few others, he would mention it felt like unseen hands were pulling him out of the woods since he did not have the strength to make it out on his own.

In what seemed like a short amount of time, Billy broke through the tree line covered in blood, sweat, and earth and wrapped in briars. He continued moving out and away from the woods into the open field.

After a few dozen feet, he moved no more and his movement forward halted. He rolled over onto his back, and looked up into the sky so thankful he was no longer in the woods. It was still such a long way across the field, it might as well have been a hundred miles. Out in the open field with no cover, the air temperature was freezing and its chill added to his misery. Lying still, Billy considered it maybe ok to let go. Billy was exhausted. He wanted to relax and just let himself go to sleep. Letting go would be peaceful. He could be rid of the crushing chest pain and cold air gripping his body.

He remembered the children who had just lit up his life and how they were waiting on him somewhere up ahead. Billy would not give up. With nothing but empty sky to look at and the earth spinning under him, he felt as if were falling through the open sky just tumbling forever into the blue vastness above him. His coat had practically been torn off him while he moved across the forest floor. Billy was shocked to see what had become of his once clean, dry, blue coat. All that remained was a tattered rag covered in mud, moss and debris held together with caked blood. The sight of his chest remained with him for many years.

He promised himself to never glance down there again.

Looking back up at the sky without the aid of a focal point, he grew increasingly worried he would not know if he had passed away. It was just open sky looking back down at him nothing to measure space with. He turned his head slightly to the side looking to find the tree line trying to keep his chest out of sight. He could use the trees to measure space with and not the vast void of empty sky. He would use the distant trees as an anchor to hold onto.

Again, the familiar voice of his guardian interrupted the silence. It was not of this world. Here in the open field Billy knew no one stood near him; yet quietly it said, "Call for help,"

Though he was bleeding to death and suffocating from the hole in his chest with his body racked in pain from uncontrolled shivering, Billy let out cries for help. He had made a terrible choice even though he was living in daily fear of the one person he looked to for love and protection. It was only temporary. He had felt and seen a future day promising joy and love. Holding onto these two ideas, he continued to frantically call out for help while focusing on the woods. While an unseen presence stood vigil over Billy, it was encouraging him to go on. While the measure of time had been reduced to taking his next breath, it was there watching over him. Billy didn't hear his protector speak anymore on that day, but he knew it was there with him. It stood with him. Surely God answered his prayer and indeed sent him an angel to protect him. God wanted him to hold fast to the promise he had been given and not lose hope while laying in that field as his life continued to spill out. The joy he had in his heart was a life jacket in an empty ocean waiting for rescue. He tried to stop thinking about the mess his chest was or falling through the sky. He turned his thoughts to fishing, tents made up of blankets, and holding someone who offered him love without condition

Letting go of the anchor the trees offered, he looked back up at the sky, and with all the strength he could summon, he continued to yell for help into blue sky.

Starting to feel as if he were lighter than air, somewhere inside of him it felt like something was trying to detach from his physical body. This was a new feeling and if he wanted to live another day, this was not a good feeling. Ignoring it, he cried out as if he did not have the hole in his chest. Time was running out. Deep from in his well of life, he lowered the bucket as far as it would go and drew deep down and let out a yell one last time, "For God's sake! Someone please help me!"

This time he felt vibrations through the ground and the unmistakable sound of footsteps running towards him. Turning his head to the side, he saw his frantic brother running towards him.

Billy moaned, "Please get help. I've shot myself and I don't want to die"

Danny looked as if here were looking at a ghost. At that moment he grew up and was no longer a child. Danny turned and with the flight of a bird took off to get help.

At this point all Billy could do was lay there and concentrate on staying awake. He missed the reassuring sound of the voice and though he could no longer hear it, he knew it was still there. Billy knew very large arms held him, now. There would be days in the future when he would feel alone, when it felt like life was crashing over him all at once and he would take a moment and pause and reflect how heaven opened up and an angel came to his aid. Heaven had moved on a simple prayer. Billy was permitted by free will to depress the trigger, but an angel was sent to intervene from that point on.

His eyes were heavy afraid if he closed them he would never wake back up. Hoping help would come quickly with his coat barely on and his shirt soaked through with blood in the open field on that winter evening, his body was racked with shivering.

Hearing the sound of more footsteps running, he turned his head to the side as he barely made out the sight of his grandfather. He ran to his grandson as if he ran with the strength of a man half his age. He had never seen his grandfather move faster than a shuffle maybe a slow walk on a good day. He wanted to smile when he saw his grandfather run towards him and everything happening to him, he saw another example of the forces working for him.

His grandfather got to his side and knelt down. He laid Billy's head in his lap and stroked his head; he told his grandfather what he had done he was sorry.

"Help is coming. I called the ambulance and they'll be here soon son. Stay here don't go. Danny was watching cartoons like he always does after school. In the middle of the cartoons, he just walked outside to do chores. He had an urgent need to come down here to stack firewood. That's how he found you."

"I don't want to be alone Granddad. I don't want to die today."

"I think you're going to be ok. I'm here with you and I'm not going anywhere. The ambulance will be here soon. Son, I don't believe you will die today. I don't believe he even put a coat on as he practically ran out of the house to go stack firewood in the back field. No sir, there is someone working to keep you here with us today."

His grandfather took his coat off, and covered Billy up and went back to cradling his head. Thankful for the warmth of his grandfather, Billy knew help was coming, but the ambulance station was a volunteer station. It was ten miles from his home along a winding country road. If the station was empty that day, he would have to wait for the volunteers to arrive at the station to start towards him. Billy hoped the volunteers were there when they received the call for help. Once the ambulance got to him, it would be another twenty minutes to get to the county hospital.

Despite the growing list of miracles Billy could anchor hope to, there was growing doubt in his mind the ambulance would not be able to get him to the hospital in time. Billy knew he was starting to run on empty like a car running low on gas any moment it would just shut off and the motor would sit lifeless. Resting in his grandfather's he drifted into a black void.

Shivering Billy woke up to the sight of a brown uniformed pant leg as a deputy sheriff stood over him. He knelt down and looked straight into Billy's eyes and asked, "Did you do this to yourself son?"

"Yes, sir," he acknowledged to the deputy.

Billy must have looked like he was only moments away from death because of the look on the deputy's face. With no concept of time and feeling like he was sliding back into that void, he tried to claw away way from it. He was not afraid of it and though it seemed like an inviting place to go, he had things to do. Billy was going to be a dad and he was not going to die on that frozen ground. The struggle was put behind him when he felt vibrations in the ground as heavy wheels drew close to him and the smell of hot exhaust reached him.

While the ambulance's diesel engine idled a few feet away, Billy started to feel something inside of him trying to unhinge or detach from his body. The ambulance, crew and ground were far away though they were working in a rush around him. A man with a large box sat down next to him. Billy felt this man roll his body over and his rough hands went up along his back. The ground was cold again, the man's rough hands and the smell of hot exhaust told Billy everything was where it was supposed to be. He was no longer far away.

"No exit wound!"

The ambulance staff started their efforts. Billy was thankful to feel the cold air around him and hear the sounds of the rumbling ambulance engine with the smell of its exhaust. Billy was still there whispering pleas to not let him die. It was urgent he make it through this day. He wanted to see the next day.

Billy looked into the face of the man looking for the exit wound and asked him to promise him he would not die. The man tried to promise Billy he would make it, but his eyes told a different story. What Billy saw in this man's eyes told him it would be close, he may not make it.

The paramedic must have known his eyes gave him away. He looked into Billy's eyes and told him with honesty "We are doing everything we can"

Billy felt himself picked up and placed on a cot followed by the sensation of being lifted up into the back of a warm ambulance. Again, the darkness swallowed him.

Billy saw light. Exhausted and not wanting to leave this peaceful quiet place and go back to the harsh world going on around his body. There sitting next to him was a beautiful woman. Though his vision was cloudy and he had a hard time seeing her, there was no doubt she was there with him. Her hair was red and it was pulled back. She had freckles and her smile sparkled. She wore a blue sweatshirt with an ambulance logo on the front and she held his hand. The sound of the siren, the motion of the ambulance and the voices of the other crew members were distant and seemingly miles away. Her voice was close at hand. There was a beaming glow around her as Billy tried to blink and bring her into focus. Nothing surprised Billy anymore today.

She could have been an angel. She did not sound like the angel who had spoken to him in the woods. She reached out, blotted his eye with some gauze and smiled. She may not be one of the angels stepping out of heaven to intervene on his behalf but she was a volunteer ambulance member to render service. Billy was so thankful to have her next to him, whoever she was, her touch and smile would be something he would remember for many years.

"Hi, Billy, you're still here. We're almost there; just a little bit further."

Despite the commotion going on around him, it was just the two of them in an isolated time on board the speeding ambulance. The incredible pressure on his chest made him want to let go; he was tired of not being able to breathe. Trying to ignore his shattered body he kept his gaze on her. She was beautiful and if these were his final moments he would be fortunate to have such a kind person in his company. Billy didn't want her to let go of his hand.

"Hard to breathe," Billy whispered.

"I know, sweetheart. I need you to not give up. Focus on

breathing, I know it's hard. Not much longer until we are at the County

Hospital, ok?"

"Ok" Billy whispered through the oxygen mask

She asked, "What grade are you in?"

"Tenth grade"

"Where do you go to school?" she continued to hold his gaze

and would not let go.

"Park City High School"

The ambulance siren whaled as they bounced, rattled and sped

towards the county hospital. Billy was not afraid of what he saw in her

eyes unlike the other's eyes. Whatever was going to happen to him he

would be ok. She was gone, darkness returned. Peace. Quiet. Still.

CHAPTER SEVEN

An explosion of movement and cold air as his body was moved. What sounded like a large door whisked open followed by warmth and the smell of antiseptics drew him from the peaceful quiet place. Bright lights from above clipped past. The sensation of being hurriedly pushed along a hallway jumbled sounds of commotion going on around him. People yelled directions at one another.

Being dragged off the cot and onto a bed, he felt like a specimen on a petri dish being prepared to go under a microscope. No more gentle hands holding his hands. These hands worked at a fevered pitch as scissors cut away his blood soaked parka then cut away his muddy pants. A cold metal slab slid under his back while big blocky machines appeared over him along with bright lights and people wearing aprons.

He heard sounds of clicks then the metal slab slid away from his back. People huddled around him. He realized he was in a large room in the county emergency room. He saw the lady from the ambulance in between the people standing around him while he was on the table. She smiled at him, turned and disappeared from sight. Billy wanted to thank her, but she was gone.

Billy did not like this room; it had only one purpose. The events getting ready to play out in this room would decide where he would wake up in the next few minutes. Would he wake up on the other side of life or in another room in the hospital recovering from this wound? How many other souls went under those bright lights while hands probed, cut, tore and fought to bring them back to this side? As the staff started to cut into his chest, Billy knew he had to be strong at this moment. Over the chaotic noise in the room he remembered the joy he felt in the woods at the sound of the children. Billy would continue to fight on and not stay far away when he felt like he was drifting away again.

A voice warned others "Hold him down. This is going to hurt!"

Heavy hands grabbed his legs and arms. He could not move when suddenly a dreadful pressure and burning sensation went into his side. He moaned and resisted, but the hands would not let him move. While the staff worked on Billy he tried to focus on the sweet sounds he heard in the woods. He tried to imagine what those children looked like with the sun shining off their faces. Billy saw a little girl splash in a pool on a hot summer day. He wanted to soak his feet in that warm water and to be away from this place.

There was no measure of time anymore. There was a distant, violent sensation of hands thrusting feverishly against the center of his chest. Billy wanted to leave this room and to get off the table and run away from those hands. Billy wanted to stay in the warm sun and soak his feet in the water. It was really not necessary for them to do this anymore. This room was cold and impersonal. Bad things were happening to his body and he wanted them to stop he wanted to spend time in the warm sun. Billy wanted to leave this room, but the hands working on him would not let him leave. What they were doing to his chest seemed to be more traumatic and violent than what the gunshot had done, but they were working hard to keep him from leaving that room. The sun was warm. The water was perfect and Billy was at home.

The curtain on that moment went down and the gym lights were slowly turned back down. The winter's night returned to the windows high above.

Erika whispered in his ear, "Thank you. That is what I really wanted tonight. We can leave now if you want."

Jumping at the invitation Erika had offered; he wasted no time taking her hand and leaving the dance floor to say a few brief goodbyes and collect their coats.

Bill had enough. It was time to say goodbye to these ghosts from his past. Reaching the gym door; he held the door open for Erika. As she walked out, he turned for one last look into the gym like that day twenty two years ago. This time instead of seeing young teens excited about what life held for them in the coming years, middle aged people lingered longer on the road of memory lane happy to once more to be prowling the halls and classes of their school. His walk down memory lane had been a private memory. Just like then, he had spent the evening alone, isolated from them in his thoughts. There was little he could add to any of the conversations flowing around him. They discussed past sports glories, high school romances, and long retired teachers. Some teachers were toasted over glasses of wine while others were voted down in shame forever holding titles to a variety of unflattering slang names. They shared how they invested money. Many were esteemed in their differing fields of endeavors.

Bill's peers would have recoiled in horror if he shared with them this story. Surely this was neither the place nor time to have shared such a story as this: memories of an angel voice, the ferocious sound of a gunshot against a still wood and through the fog of death the sounds of his children playing twenty years before their birthday. Not light dinner conversation to share with people not seen in twenty years. One last glance at his former class, he was proud of their success. He only wished he had been as equally successful as they were.

CHAPTER EIGHT

Whispering goodbye to them and to his memories, he turned and walked out the door. Bill let the door slam shut heavily behind him. It was time to go home. If he got home in time he would be able to catch the kids still up much to Erika's displeasure. He would have time to entertain Anna with the Silly Brown Bear Gang. Bedtime was an important time in their home and the Silly Brown Bear Gang made an appearance every night to tuck Anna in. The babysitter Ms. Belinda would not understand or be able to do the Silly Brown Bear Gang routine.

Cleaning off the light snow and turning the ignition switch on. The motor turned over and the motor valve tap slapped him back to reality. It had only been a few hours since Erika complained to him the hairdryer was broken and needed to be replaced. He was being pulled in two. If a broken hair dryer was all it took to put their week's finances into a spiral, where would he get the money for an expensive motor repair or a car payment on a new car? His peers seemed to be confident, successful and could afford to replace a broken hair dryer. If they needed to fix their car, they fixed it. If they needed a new car, they bought it. He hated to struggle all the time. He was tired of not providing a nice family vacation. They were missing out on life. What was the point of being blessed with this family if his life was being drained by the constant worry of putting food on the table and a roof over their head? There was little time to just sit and enjoy the gift he had been given. He worked hard and stretched every dollar as far as it would go. If the van went anytime soon, they were going to be in trouble.

The van was warm enough and Bill put it in drive and coasted past the many new and expensive-looking parked cars. As they left the parking lot, Erika tried making small talk to occupy their trip home. It was a very one-sided conversation:

After a few miles she interrupted her own thought and blurted out, "Would you like to talk about it?"

"Sure, I hated it," Bill replied.

"Thanks," she said hurt.

"No, that's not what I meant. I did enjoy being out with you. Listen to the van. Its dying and I don't have the money to fix it. The hairdryer is broken, so in order for me to give you money to buy one, we will have to take away from grocery money this week."

"Hair dryers are not expensive."

Bill sighed. She was going to make him work to explain himself. He wished this would be one of those times in their years of marriage her experience with him would lend aid so she would understand what he was trying to get off his chest.

"It's not the hairdryer. It's not this old van were driving. What kind of provider am I for you and the kids? Is our financial situation so delicate a busted hair dryer puts us in a downward spiral? We have to decide between you going with wet hair for the week or no laundry detergent." Bill paused trying to focus on his words and the road ahead.

"I'm a failure. I lay shingles for a living. I never went to school and if I had, I could earn a better life for us. What accomplishment in my life can I be proud of or can my kids be proud of me and say 'dad did that'? Who wants to listen to my story of hauling shingles up a roof or doing a carpet install as a side job with your brother to make extra money? The vacation last year was in the back yard watching the kids splash in the pool we bought from the "Everything under a Buck Store". *That* was the highpoint for the year"

The air in the van was icy cold, and it was not from the cold winter night air or how long it was taking the van to warm the air inside.

Erika had a reply for her husband, the truth hurt, "Bill, I like to hear about your day. I know the kids love to hear you sit and talk to them. You were the creator of the Silly Brown Bear gang and your daughter enjoys that more than any cartoon on TV. Tell her you're a failure one day because you don't work in an office and wear a tie with your name on a desk." Erika was just warming up and the truth was already starting to have a sting to it. Erika looked straight ahead and continued on," I think you're being hard on yourself if you hold

yourself up to those standards trying to measure your life worth and

success by how much you paid for our vacation last year. If you think

spending time soaking your feet in your daughter's cheap plastic pool is

a waste, then yes, by those measures your life was a waste. I would say

we are blessed and wealthy. We have seventeen years of precious

memories with three wonderful babies who love and adore us. We

struggle to keep the basics under the roof and there is rarely any left

over for extras in life, but we are always provided for. We have more

love in our home than most people will ever have in a lifetime. In my

life, I've never doubted your ability to provide for the kids and me. I'm

sorry if you think your life has been a waste."

Bill knew he had said too much; it was time to open mouth and

insert foot. Something bothered him and he struggled to get it out. It

was a question something was trying to lay on his heart. Being given

another chance at life was no light matter. Ever since that day he

wanted to be a good steward with the life he was given. Bill always felt

he was going to rise to great things after narrowly escaping that moment in the woods. The only thing he rose to in his opinion was hoisting another load of shingles on top of a hot roof. Erika sat far enough away from him in the van there would be no chance of her leg accidentally brushing against his.

Lying in the hospital bed a few days after the shooting, he watched a national tragedy unfold on TV high above the sky. With no warning, an explosion lit up the TV on a live broadcast and brave astronauts perished shortly after they took off. Billy felt a connection to them. Every day, there was news of some person dying but never before did he feel a sense of knowing. Watching the plume of debris fall from the sky he remembered his time in the trauma room downstairs and how the efforts of those hands kept from leaving the room. Those brave souls had gone further than he had and all day long they showed the explosion on the TV. Nurses and doctors came into his room and spoke of the tragedy. He wanted to tell the staff to turn the TV off every time they replayed the explosion, and watching those astronauts die, he could feel his time in the field and in the trauma room. That night while the nation mourned, nightmares interrupted his sleep. Again there was the shot, the flash, followed by the bitter smell of gun powder and the sweet aroma of blood. For many nights, these nightmares haunted his sleep to the point Billy was afraid to sleep.

The day after the national tragedy high above the sky, the surgeon came to see him off. Close instructions were given to help heal his body. Medicines were prescribed to reduce the pain in his chest; pain he would felt the rest of his life. After instructions were given on how the body would heal, the surgeon paused and looked Billy in the eyes. The surgeon wanted him to know he had been fortunate. The surgeon worked feverishly and skillfully and kept Billy in that room. Looking like a scarecrow, he was pushed out of the hospital in a wheelchair.

The nightmares continued while he was at home. From his bedroom window, the shadow of the woods was not far away. Memories of the hands working on his chest in a violent manner and the sensation of the blast would wake him up causing him to want to leap out of the bed. The woods were so close to him. They were cold, dark and empty.

CHAPTER NINE

A week after being home and being tormented by the nightmares, the telephone rang one afternoon. On the other end of the line was a friendly lady who had a message for Billy. She was the mother of a girl who sat behind him in his home room class. Billy had never spoken to her before. She sounded awkward on the phone. She asked if she could forward a message to Billy.

"It was crazy," she said. She went on to tell Billy, "I was vacuuming my home, and above the sound of my very old, very loud vacuum, I heard a voice call out to me. I had to shut the vacuum cleaner off. I had never heard this before. It spoke to me! I am sure your thinking who is this crazy lady? Billy you have never been in my thoughts before. I know this must be awkward for you but I have to tell you this. Well, it wanted me to tell you God loved you and He has his hand on you and to not be afraid. He is with you. He wants me to come see you one day if that's ok?" Her family would become one of his closest friends in life. .

One night after his new friend had come to visit Billy; she encouraged him to pray like he did in the woods if he was ever afraid of the dark and nightmares kept him from resting. That night, Billy closed his eyes again and prayed to God telling him he was tired and afraid to sleep. He was afraid of the things he would see while he slept. A familiar presence came into his room and drove back the fear of the night. His angel was there still watching over him while he slept and continued to intervene in his life. Sleep was restful and there was no more fear of the woods.

Billy's father would never put his hands on him again after that time. No more being shut away in a room for days on end to sit in a chair. He would see a person once a week for about a year to help him sort through things. They wanted to make sure this would never happen again and it didn't. The person there to help him sort through things never talked with him about the vivid images haunting his thoughts. What this person failed to help him heal from, the passage of time did. With the passing of years the shot was not as loud, the pain of not being able to breathe, or the hands keeping him from the table faded away and were less intense in detail.

What did replace his every waking thought was the beautiful girl he met at a pancake breakfast benefit and how lovely she looked on the day they were married. Bill put Billy behind him and went about finding employment and buying his new wife a couch to put in their first apartment. They bought their first car together and soon their home. By the time Erika came into their bedroom to tell him the news there would be an addition to their family those memories were all but gone. Diapers, electric bills and cleaning up melted ice cream cones off of little shirts took up his thoughts. Life had moved on.

Life had started to bury Bill as he got older. The overwhelming sense of not being able to meet their needs robbed him of his joy for life. The violent memories had been forgotten; however, also forgotten was he had been given a second chance at life. Bill forgot the solemn words from the surgeon trying to impress on him, he was as lifeless as one could be without being gone forever. Not many were afforded that opportunity, be a good steward of this gift.

Sitting at a traffic light, listening to the tap in the motor he was allowing it to steal his joy. He didn't have an interesting life to regal people at a dinner table. Is this what his life had been reduced to: constant worry over just keeping an existence? Erika was right they had scratched out an existence for years, and they always had enough.

As the light turned green, Bill knew he was at a familiar point in his life. This time instead of hearing a question posed to him in his ear, he felt its burdening weight on his heart. He had lost his way once again and he was in danger of losing his life again. Maybe not immediately, but the sort of loss of life occurs over weeks, months and years while taking for granted things that mattered. While driving home after those memories visited him, Bill knew he had been close to crossing over that day. The actions of the surgeons in the trauma room kept him from leaving the table and leaving the room. He had been held to this side of life by a thin thread. Knowing what the surgeon wanted him to know, during those moments as the frantic work went on around him not one time did his thoughts consider the worries of this world. The only thought that drove his purpose to live was the thought of sharing love with those who would call him: dad.

He had offered a plea to God to protect him and send him an Angel once before. God had answered even though it was not a one-time deal. Here today, with the company of his beautiful wife he was deeply in love with, the only thing he had moaned about was broken appliances, a dying van and being in an uncomfortable social situation. His life was passing him by. What precious fleeting moments have been lost never to be gotten back pressed heavily in Bill's soul.

Pulling into the driveway and shutting the van off, Erika got out frustrated her night was not what it could have been. Watching her go inside their little home and shut the door, she left him outside in the cold winter night. The warm glow of light coming through the window was inviting. This was their little home. There were the small trees they had planted a couple of years ago. A sign hung from the door welcoming friends. Looking in the rearview mirror Bill saw his kid's empty car seats.

The question burdening his heart on the way home became clear. His life was a few dozen feet from him in that little home. Bill once wished he had the life of the kids preparing to attend the important title basketball game. Bill wanted to live in a house and not be afraid. Again in the gym once more with many of the same people from twenty years ago he was envious of their life once again. The question became clear and the haze of sorting things through cleared out and a single thought came to Bill "would you exchange the life you have been given for another?"

His heart's desire had been granted. It was his life, the tragedy of that day when he turned a rifle on himself to escape his fear and the joy the first time he felt a small foot kick inside of Erica as he felt life growing in her. "I would not trade places with anyone. I am a blessed man and it is good to be alive."

Opening the door to the van and walking across the snowy driveway and pausing, he could hear the sound of children's voices all waiting to see their daddy. Bedtimes were important in this house and it was his time with the kids. It was the time when the Silly Brown Bear Gang tucked them in. Bill would gladly take a lifetime of broken down vans to have a life of nights with his wife and the Silly Brown Bear Gang. Bill turned the door knob and went through the door. Shrieks broke out as Anna yelled for her daddy as she bounded across the living room towards her father. She was followed closely by Brady: he tried to keep up but he tripped and landed hard. He started to cry out for his daddy. He hugged Anna and kissed her on the cheek and bent down and picked up Brady and held him until the tears went away. Erika was beautiful holding Cayden; whose face was covered in a teething cookie.

Anna jumped into his arms covering her dad with kisses and asking, "Daddy, do we have time for the Silly Brown Bear Gang to come out and play and tuck me in?"

"Yes, sweetheart, there is time for the bears to tuck you in; they wouldn't miss it for anything."

"OK guys, thank Ms. Belinda for coming over to watch you and give mommy kisses goodnight."

Anna went to Ms. Belinda and thanked her for sharing her cookies and told her mom she loved her and kissed her goodnight. Bill went to Erika and took Cayden. Holding Cayden and whispering "contact" making a propeller sound as Bill and his youngest son took off together. From somewhere a familiar memory, a propeller caused the two of them to gain loft as they soared together towards the sky. He loved being a father.

Reaching the landing he heard a small little girl's voice call down the hall after him the bears were ready to tuck her in. He saw a small pajama covered rear end of a two year old boy disappear around the corner running into his room laughing as he ran. He went to the boy's room and put the smallest in his crib forgetting to clean the cookie off his son's face. He plucked up the two year old and lightly jogged out of the boy's room and headed down the hall to an anxiously waiting four year old little girl. The Silly Brown Bear Gang came out as a vivid bedtime story unfolded complete with the few small bears, a stuffed frog and a stuffed cow. Lots of hugs and kisses were shared between a dad and his kids. He turned off her light and tucked his son

his bed. Going into the hallway, Bill bowed his head and whispered a

word of thanksgiving for the life he had been given. Bill knew he was

provided for. If God cared enough to send an angel to intervene and

save his life surely he would provide for all of their needs.

THE END

CPSIA information can be obtained
at www.ICGtesting.com
Printed in the USA
BVOW06s0855200317
478937BV00015B/291/P